You don't want dessert, do you?

Using humor, entertainment, education and training to create a customer service experience that enriches your customers' lives.

Frank Lanzkron-Tamarazo

DEDICATION

To my wife, Lisa, who has been my loving partner during this joyous life.

To my children, Max, Doris, and Nicoletta, who have enjoyed discussing and living through the horrible dining experiences more than the great ones.

Most of all, I dedicate this book to the numerous servers and customer service representatives who have enriched my life, created peace in my world, and taught me that deeds of loving kindness are limitless.

YOU DON'T WANT DESSERT, DO YOU?

CUSTOMER SERVICE MENU

ACKNOWLEDGMENTS

I have great gratitude for some more than memorable managers and owners, Fred from Chi-Chi's Mexican Restaurant on Staten Island, Ron, the owner of The Rustic Inn in Annapolis, Luigi from Lucky's Bar and Grill in Manhattan, and Luciano Del Signore, the chef/ owner of Bacco Ristorante in Southfield, Michigan.

Robert Palmer of Raven Writing Studios encouraged and assisted with the writing of this book and the many other books to come.

Many thanks to the television personalities: Chef Gordon Ramsey of "Kitchen Nightmares" and Charles Stiles of "Mystery Diners." The entertaining and sometime gruesome situations during their shows helped recall many of the stories in this book. Our family is obsessed with these two shows.

Thank you to the most important editor, my wife, Lisa, who is the most honest person that I know.

Introduction

Why write this book?

We loved the restaurant. It was crowded and noisy. That's just how we like it. We're two twenty-somethings in love. The expensive red wine and the conversation was flowing. It's that magical time, before kids, in New York City. We gorged ourselves on breaded zucchini with fresh parmigiano reggiano cheese sprinkled lovingly and mozzarella sticks with the best marinara dip possible. Our eyes were locked and no one else existed. We're two happy college kids with a restaurant bill well over $50. With hundreds of other dining choices around us on the Upper West Side, we chose to dine in this restaurant once, sometimes, twice weekly. When it was time for the server to ask us about dessert, he dropped the check on the table, and said, "You don't want dessert, do you?" Shocked and amused, we said, "Why, yes, we do want dessert." The memorable dessert arrived. Despite our usual overzealous tipping tradition, we left one dollar for the lousy service throughout the meal. The waiter's question, "You don't want dessert, do you?" is the name of this book because it captures the essence of bad service perfectly.

Over the last 20 years, I have calculated with great trepidation, that we've dined out at least 5 times each month, for a total of...you do the math. I would probably lose my sanity if I guessed how much my enjoyment of life has cost me over my short lifetime. This book is the culmination of how Lisa and I (and now our children) have analyzed and judged our customer service experiences. Whenever we dine out either in fine dining, diners or coneys (I've lived in Michigan for awhile now), burger joints, or fast food chains, our family has established a baseline for analyzing whether the experience has enriched our lives, made us laugh in shock or disgust, and whether the establishment is poised to fail.

My wife, Lisa, and I have had wonderful and terrible service at restaurants, but "You don't want dessert, do you?" is the worst question we've heard at a restaurant in our lives. The question summarizes many of the topics in my book. I want to help you, the diner, server, manager or owner, start a dining revolution. For the servers, I want to teach you what you don't know and what your managers may never teach you. I want you to excel and create more wealth for yourself. Your knowledge about customer service will help you become an owner, manager, politician, or stay at home parent. For the manager or owner, I want to teach you how to train your employees. With all of your many responsibilities, training employees every day is burdensome, but crucial to the continued health and survival of your business. If you give up on teaching even the mundane, you've given up. Attention to detail and reinvention of how you sell and provide excellent customer service needs to be reborn every day.

If you believe that your customer service skills are great, please read this book anyway. If you own, manage, or work in a restaurant or café, you're featured in this book. My wife and I are classical singers. As a singer, if you listen to yourself sing while you're singing, you're probably not singing well. When we sing, the sound that we hear is inaccurate because we're hearing the sound in our own heads, not what the listener hears. Singers are properly taught to sing by sensation, not by hearing. And when vocal problems develop by over exertion or stress, it is very difficult to cure those ills. We need a vocal coach, a skilled teacher who is objective, to assist with our return to healthy singing. Sometimes, singers destroy their voices with poor technique and never recover their voices or careers.

The singer's life is similar to the restaurant or café experience. For many restaurants, cafés, or any customer service environment, you often fail to evaluate your operating procedures unless you're in deep financial trouble; by that time, it's often too late. Once you fall into a deep abyss of terrible customer service, there may come a point of no return.

When I was a teen, I worked for Chi-Chi's Mexican Restaurant on Staten Island as a busboy and runner. I was then trained to wait tables, host, and finally to tend bar. In Manhattan, I was a server at Lucky's Bar and Grill, an upscale eatery on 6th avenue. At the famed Tavern on the Green in Central Park, I was a host. In Annapolis, Maryland, I was a server for a fine dining establishment, The Rustic Inn. The managers at all of these restaurants are featured in this book. In all of these jobs, I was blessed to have someone who actively trained me to be the best. I was instructed in hard work, rewards for doing a great job, and techniques for great customer service. The managers and owners taught me the good, the bad, and the ugly of great customer service.

At Chi-Chi's, I learned about great customer service and about integrity. The managers at Lucky's taught me about the importance of constant training of your staff. The Rustic Inn taught me about educating customers and adding value to the experience with entertainment and knowledge of the menu. All of these experiences taught me about how to create superior customer service standard operating procedures for my business, Chazzano Coffee Roasters. My café was the testing ground and reality check for all that is written in this book.

The life of a synagogue Cantor is one of the most difficult customer service jobs. In Hebrew, the Cantor is considered a "holy vessel," "a servant of Israel (Jews)." A clergy person is constantly in customer service mode. In order to engage and serve your people, you need to entertain, educate, amuse, and create interesting content. It's impossible to please everyone and sometimes you feel as if you are pleasing no one.

The Top 10 Recurring Events that make this book necessary:

1. You fill the ice bin. You grab a bag of ice from the freezer and then...drop it on the floor in order to break up the ice cubes. Really? You just dropped a bag of ice, wrapped in easy to rip plastic, on the floor. Now there are holes in the bag and the ice is mixing with whatever is on the dirty floor. Watching and hearing the bag slammed on the floor horrifies me.

2. Using a glass to scoop out ice. I was once served a tall glass of soda at a high-end fish restaurant with, wait for it...a large shard of broken glass.

3. Stacking Plates at the table. Even my Italian grandmother wouldn't stack plates at the table.

4. Passing plates of food to customers and expecting them to take it from you, especially when you have ample space to go around them. Then the server says, "Be careful, hot plate," and hands it to me.

5. Reaching across a customer to serve the person next to them.

6. "Selling" the menu. "Who had the Penne Arrabiata?" "Eggplant Parmigian'?" I feel like I'm at an auction and I fear that you have dementia. You are serving two tables and you can't remember what I ordered.

7. Passing by my table when you're in the "weeds" without looking at me. The spicy enchilada is delicious, but I will probably need an emergency refill of my beverage soon. I

may not even have utensils with which to eat my delicious food, but you keep passing my table. Are you ignoring me?

8. You make me wait for a very long time after serving dessert to give me a check. Or, I wait for an eternity before you acknowledge my existence.

9. I ordered the French Fries, you don't bring it to the table, and then you argue with me, "You didn't order the French Fries."

10. You don't know the menu. You mispronounce the menu items and you need to ask the chef to answer every simple question posed.

These events occurred because the server hasn't been trained in the art of customer service. If you learn anything from this book, please remember that training never ends. Even if you trained your staff to repair those ten pet peeves, I hope that you understand that effective training is like whack-a-mole. Solve one problem and then something new and damaging to the business will emerge.

I am writing this book for selfish reasons. Life is short. A great meal with great customer service enriches my life. I created Chazzano Coffee Roasters because very few of our dining experiences ended on a high note with an awesome cup of coffee. I suppose that all of my books are based on my selfish motives, but I hope that this one will improve your life and business.

1

Three ingredients necessary for a successful sale

Humor, creativity, and hunger for a sale are the three ingredients necessary for a successful sale.

Humor: a comic, absurd, or incongruous quality causing amusement

In my opinion, humor is the single most important ingredient for any job or for any friendship. There are many lovely people in the world who weren't born with the gene for humor. I will always be nice to them, but they won't be my dearest friends. Humor allows us to get through the darkest times in our lives. In a restaurant and café atmosphere, humor allows us to entertain our customers and help them forget their troubles. However, too much humor is annoying. Customers don't want to be part of a comedy routine unless they're actually at a comedy show. At Chazzano Coffee Roasters, we're known for saying that if you put sugar or cream in our coffee, "God cries and an angel loses its wings." That's not outrageously funny, but it brings a smile to our customer's face and adds value to our product.

If you are a regular speaker in front of groups, the best opening is a humorous ice breaker. Whenever I speak in front of small or large groups, I agonize about what I will say to make my listeners laugh or smile in the first few seconds. Happy people are better listeners and better consumers. What can you say to your diners when you approach the table for the first time? Is there something humorous about your menu? If your restaurant has 50 different beers from which to choose, I would suggest saying, "I know that there aren't enough choices." That may make them smile and then your next question will be, "What kind of beer do you like, a stout, IPA, lager, dark beer, light beer?" Then you can suggest your personal favorite. If you use some additional humor by suggesting a beer that has a humorous name, like Dirty Bastard, or other somewhat lightly inappropriate name, you've just entertained them with your wit and joy of life.

When someone asks me about a particular single serve coffee maker or an old fashioned drip maker, I'll joke: "You should bring your coffee maker to the police, along with your guns. Or donate it to someone you dislike. It doesn't make a great cup of coffee." Choose humor that supports the branding of the business. Ask me about Kopi Luwak, coffee harvested from the feces of a particular Asian palm civet, I'll quickly say, "Why would I want to drink crappy coffee?"

It's important to always be equipped with your sense of humor. Life is short. When I was a waiter in Annapolis, Maryland, a customer believed that her wine glass was leaking. I knew that the wine glass wasn't leaking, but I smiled and apologized and brought her another one. If you find the humor in others, you're able to serve them better. If I stated, "Ma'am, the glass isn't leaking, you're just dribbling wine down the glass," I wouldn't last long in that job and wouldn't have received a great tip.

Find the humor in everything that you do, and you'll live with less stress and greater happiness.

It's important to have a smile on your face, not manufactured, but coming from true happiness that you have a job, enjoy your job, and are living a beautiful life.

Creativity: Do you have Vegetarian Rennet? No.

Me: "Do you have vegetarian rennet?"

Cashier: "No."

Recently, my son, Max, and I walked into two health food stores. We wanted to make homemade Mozzarella cheese and rennet is a necessary enzyme for the forming of this cheese. Regular rennet that comes from the marrow of non-Kosher animals isn't possible for observant Jews. Therefore, we needed to find vegetarian rennet that is a good kosher substitute. At the first store, I waited patiently for a cashier to notice me. She then turns to me without a smile. I asked the question with a smile on my face. She answered, curtly, "No," and then turned towards another customer. Then we walked across the street to another health food store and asked two unfriendly owners the same question: "Do you carry vegetarian rennet?" The store was completely empty except for Max and me and they, too, said "No."

In Judaism, it is believed that when one attends Rosh Hashanah services and hears the sounding of the shofar, that the ancient musical instruments can literally change the name and attributes of G-d. G-d's name changes dramatically from a G-d of Judgment to a G-d of Compassion. Words and music are powerful. In the same way, there are words to change a new customer into a life-long customer.

Here is a possible dialog that would have changed me forever.

Health Food Store Employee (HFSE)- (with a smile) Hi, how are you? I'll be right with you.

Me: Great. Thank you.

HFSE: (after a few minutes) I apologize. How may I help you?

Me: Do you have vegetarian rennet?

HFSE: Rennet? No, we don't carry that product. Have you checked at the Health Food Store across the street, yet?

Me: No, not yet.

HFSE: Wait a moment. Let me ask my manager if we've sold rennet in the past. He may be able to order it for you. I'll be right back.

Me: Awesome. Thank you.

(A few minutes later the HFSE brings her manager)

HFSManager: Hello (w/ a big smile on his face) Sorry, we don't carry vegetarian rennet for some reason, but we can have Sarah (the HFSE) order it for you and we'll call you when it's ready. Is that okay?

Me: That's great. Thank you very much.

Sarah: That rennet will cost $X. What is your name, phone number, and e-mail address?

(I provide Sarah with all of that information)

Me: Thank you very much. I need to purchase a few more

items. I'll be right back.

Coda: I leave with $100 worth of products from their store. They gained a frequent customer. The total value of my purchases if they just said, "No?" Less than $0 because I will tell (and have told) other people how poor their customer service was. The total value of an answer of "No, but let me see how we can find it for you" is more than $500 because I become a regular customer and I tell a few friends how they helped me create this homemade mozzarella.

At Chazzano Coffee Roasters, new customers ask questions that secretly hurt our souls, but we never just say "no."

New Customer: Do you have instant coffee?

Us: No. All of our coffee is fresh roasted every day. If you want coffee that's quick to make in the morning, have you used a French Press?

New Customer: I actually have a French Press in my basement that I've never used. How do you use one?

Us: (We explain how to use the French Press)

New Customer: Great. May I have 1 pound of coffee for French Press?

New Customer: Do you have Espresso Roast coffee?

Us: No, because that is a misnomer for over roasted coffee. Any coffee may be brewed for espresso as long as the flavor profile and mouthfeel are balanced. Smell this coffee (we hold open a bag of fresh roasted coffee)- this is one of our boldest coffees with notes of chocolate and almonds.

Customer: A large to go, please.

New Customer: Do you have Jamaica Blue Mountain coffee?

Us: No. There was a poor crop this year for Jamaica Blue Mountain. Would you like to try some Haiti Blue Mountain? It's the same coffee varietal, Blue Mountain, but it's grown in Haiti. The farmers receive over 300% more than the usual Fair Trade price.

New Customer: Do you have Mocha lattes?

Us: No, but our coffee is more complex than wine. If you're looking for a chocolaty latte, I would suggest the Mexico Chiapas. It has notes of rich dark chocolate when brewed in a latte. If you don't love it, it's on the house.

Customer: Do you have the Timor Leste FTO coffee?

Us: No. We should be receiving that coffee in two weeks. Would you like to try a coffee that's similar to that flavor profile?

New Customer: Do you have Hemp Milk?

Us: No, we don't. We have Almond Milk, Coconut Milk and Soy Milk. We haven't found a Hemp or Flax milk that tastes great with our coffee.

Never begin and end a sentence with "no." Don't apologize for products you don't serve, but educate your customer about the great products you serve. This approach applies to all customer service opportunities. My stomach and my father's side of my family, the Tamarazo side, are Italian. If there is a heaven, Penne Arrabbiata is served whenever I desire it. Arrabbiata means "angry." It's a spicy sauce that brings true joy to my life. Whenever I go to a nice Italian restaurant, I ask the server, "Do you have Penne Arrabbiata?" A poor server, and poor employee, will say, "No. I'm sorry that's not on the menu." She won't offer a substitute. However, the best server will say, "Let me ask the chef if she can make that for you. May I bring you some beverages while you wait?" The server speaks with the chef and returns to our table: "The chef asked, 'how hot do you want the sauce to be?'" I answer, "Thank the chef for me. I appreciate it greatly. The spiciness level is up to the chef."

Creativity in the service industry is the art of helping your customers make decisions based on their needs.

If you don't have an eggplant parmigiano hero on the menu, ask the chef if it's possible to appease the customer. I have a great sense of humor, a great deal of patience, and I enjoyed gathering the illustrative stories for this book. For those reasons, I continually call a local Italian restaurant that does not have eggplant parmigiano heroes on the menu and naturally, request one. My stomach is Italian, I grew up in an Italian-Jewish home, and my favorite sandwich is eggplant parmigiano. On the surface, it's an unremarkable dish with fried and breaded slices of eggplant, cheese, and tomato sauce. However, this isn't just a sandwich. Memories of my childhood flood my brain. When I enjoy this sandwich, I can hear the loud arguing of my Italian family, the expletives filling the air, and the laughter of my mother and my Aunt Rose.

This particular Italian restaurant has an eggplant parmigiano entree, various sandwiches on Italian bread, but they don't have an eggplant parmigiano hero. Every Italian restaurant in New York City, my homeland, has an eggplant hero on the menu. Every time I call, I have the same conversation with the manager, chef, and employee. And yes, the dialogue never really changes from week to week. In addition, I always convince them eventually to sell me a sandwich with breaded eggplant, cheese, and tomato sauce on Italian bread. Here's the dialogue:

Me: Hello. I'd like to place an order to be picked up. I'd like to order two eggplant parmigiano heroes, please.

Cashier: We don't have that on the menu. Let me ask the chef.

Chef: (Heard in the distance loudly) Tell him no!

Cashier: What do you want again?

Me: I just want the eggplant parmigiano on an Italian hero. That's all. You have Italian bread and you have eggplant parmigiano. I just want the eggplant parmigiano on top of a hero.

Cashier: Okay. Please hold on. (The cashier doesn't mute the phone, so I hear every bit of the conversation.) He says that he just wants it on Italian bread.

Chef (loudly in the distance, again) Charge him $12 for it!

Manager: (Returning to the conversation with me) Hello, this is the manager. It's just that we don't have it on our menu. Do you want cheese on your eggplant parmigiano?

Me: (screaming in my head because parmigiano is a kind of cheese) Yes, please, with tomato sauce. (with humor) I'll pay whatever you want. I'm from New York and I love eggplant parmigiano heroes.

Manager: Please hold on. I'll be right back.

Me: (waiting for five minutes until the cashier returns, I share with my children the hilarious conversation that I'm having with this restaurant)

Manager: Okay. It will be ready in 20 minutes.

When my wife and I enter the restaurant, we are not greeted warmly. After an uncomfortable silence and a secret contest of who will speak first, I say hello. Five employees pass us by as the cashier retrieves our sandwiches. No smile is found anywhere in the restaurant. The restaurant is desolate. None of the employees are rushing to complete a task. We pay, say thank you (first), and leave without any employee saying "goodbye."

Hunger for a Sale:

"You need to sell, sell, sell"

At Lucky's Bar and Grill, the manager would say to us before every shift, "You need to sell, sell, sell. It's a dog-eat-dog world out there." This was spoken after the mandatory wine tasting that would take place at every afternoon training. It was imperative that we were knowledgeable about the wines. The manager knew that knowledgeable servers sell more bottles of wine. I often won the monthly contest for the most bottles sold.

In any sales situation, you, the salesperson, must anticipate questions before they are asked. What are the possible questions that you may be asked in your profession? What are some of the normal questions as well as the crazy questions? For example, in the coffee business, customers want to know what various terms mean, Fair Trade Organic, Rainforest Alliance, Strictly High Grown, or sometimes it's the crazy questions they can't ask anywhere else like what is the coffee that the cat poops out? (Kopi Luwak)

As a restaurant server, the questions can be: Do you have gluten-free products? May I substitute another vegetable for the french fries? Or simply, what should I order? What's your favorite wine on the menu?

As a server, you are a salesperson first. Your main goal is to create more wealth for you and the restaurant. Few people work as a waiter or bartender just for the fun. What makes it worthwhile is when you're earning several hundreds of dollars in tips every shift so that you may grow your life. What are the most important questions that you are asked every shift? Memorize them and plan out your answers. Maybe you should even tell a quick and true story. Where was the fish of the day caught? What are the names of the people who own this fishery? Ask the chef questions about the specials. Why did she use that ingredient for the special? Make it personal and make the customer feel like they are part of the business. Don't talk about yourself.

The ultimate secret of selling is knowing your customers' objections even before they voice them. If you dispute their unsaid and possible objection before they voice it, you've created a new sale. For example, Chazzano Coffee Roasters does not sell inexpensive or cheap coffee. We're not expensive, but our good reputation makes people believe that we are. When I discuss the cost of a coffee that is $40 per pound, I remind my customer that a pound of coffee brews over 40 cups. Therefore, each cup of coffee costs only $1. Try to find an excellent cup of coffee anywhere for just $1! So, $24 per pound or even $32 per pound is a bargain. When I'm at a sales call at a potential wholesale account, I'll share that a particular coffee will only cost 25 cents per cup. If you sell my coffee at $2 per cup, you'll earn $1.75 per cup!

If helping a customer purchase wisely and abundantly doesn't bring you joy, get out of the service industry. To be successful, you need to be hungry for a sale.

2

How the server failed us

Let me count the ways that our server failed us today. We dined at this particular restaurant because the food was traditionally very good and it was a convenient stop on our way home from a long road trip. The only good thing during this particular visit was that the hostess greeted us warmly with a smile. The restaurant was virtually empty. After sitting at our table for five minutes, the waitress introduced herself and told us that she would return to take our order. Where was she going? There were very few people in the restaurant. A great question would've been: "May I bring some water to you while you're waiting?" She returned another five minutes later to take our order. She was pleasant, but never smiled. There were several specials on the menu. It would have been spectacular if she explained to us which menu items she loved or if she described the specials, briefly. She then took our order of 3 Mountain Dews, 1 Diet Pepsi, 3 eggplant panini, 1 cheese ravioli from the kids' menu, and a cheese tortellini, with 2 side orders of mashed potatoes, and one order each of onion rings and french fries.

Ten minutes later, the first thing to arrive is the order of onion rings and french fries. As the server is about to leave, I ask her for more napkins because my 11-year-old has just used her napkin to blow her nose and we're about to devour some greasy food with our hands. Lisa also gently reminds the server about our beverages. A few minutes later, we receive our beverages and the server asks, "Who else gets the Mountain Dew?" This is what I call, "selling" the order. When you treat the customers as the unknowing participants in a food auction. "Selling" is one of the worst sins of customer service. It wasn't a difficult order. Ten minutes ago, I had declined a beverage, and all three kids ordered the same beverage. Again, she was serving food to only two tables.

Then the rest of the food arrived. The booth has ample room for the server to move around customers. There are some cramped or small restaurants where you must pass plates across your customers. However, in this restaurant, the server had plenty room to walk around us and serve the food appropriately. Remember, serve from the left, remove from the right. Unfortunately, the server parked herself at the end of the table and attempted to hand plates to Lisa. The server was trying to use Lisa as a food runner. Lisa was not accepting the role. This forced the server to walk a few inches further to deliver the food to the proper customer. Handing plates to customers and involving them in serving their own food is another major sin.

So, what was missing? Oh yes, the two orders of mashed potatoes weren't delivered to our table, yet. As we were about to completely finish our entrees, the mashed potatoes arrived. The good news is that the mashed potatoes were then quickly ingested by three ravenous children. While I stepped away from the table for a few moments, the waitress, I am told, asked us if we were ready for the check. Another missed opportunity occurred. It reminded me of my previous story of "You don't want dessert, do you?" We were stuffed and sated, but who doesn't want dessert? If she would've asked us if we would like to see the dessert menu, she would have earned another few dollars in tips.

My wife, I knew, was parched and dying for a refill of diet soda, but with all of the many sins that we had experienced, she just couldn't ask the server for something so basic. Many times during the meal, my wife gave me "the look." You know that look of: "Really. She's doing nothing right and you're going to say something about mistake 'x'?" So, I remained silent. In addition, napkins arrived a very long time after the french fries, onion rings, and buttery eggplant panini were served.

I will never know whether the kitchen was at fault. Did the waitress place the order for onion rings and french fries before all of the other meals? Did she know that the mashed potatoes would take so long or did she forget about them?

Were the entrees sitting for 15 minutes under the heat lamp? I have no idea what happened. We would need Chef Gordon Ramsey to find out the truth.

The moral of the story is that the owners need to train their staff and they need to micromanage the dining room and kitchen. The chef needs to effectively communicate with the servers. The reason for training can be represented by a simple mathematical formula:

Great service with a smile + Great Food = increased tips and a better life.

A business person will often write down financial goals and create and test actions to achieve those goals. If you work as a server, ask yourself: What kinds of actions will help me achieve my gratuity goals? How much money in tips do I need to earn? How much money do I want to earn? If you reach certain financial goals while you improve your customer service, you will create a formula for increased revenue. If you begin to smile more often and you're receiving greater tips every shift, you'll create some benchmarks and skills that help grow your life.

Treat these customer service actions in the same way that you create an exercise program. Every shift, add another tactic, execute it consistently, and analyze its effectiveness.

Smile: Smile when you see a customer for the first time. Smile when you are taking their orders. Smile when you are serving them. Smile when they leave.

Competence: Memorize every item on the menu. Know every ingredient contained in every dish. Memorize the daily specials. In front of a mirror, practice reciting the daily specials. Smile while you are reciting the menu.

Serving dishes in the proper sequence: If you don't know which dishes should be served first, ask the chef. If you have further questions, ask the diners. Do you want the appetizers out first or the soup special?

Treat your customers like Kings and Queens: What happens when a servant passes by the King without looking at them and the King needs something? Yes, a beheading would be a pleasant punishment. When you are passing customers, look at them. If they need something, they will request it only if you acknowledge them. Better yet, plan accordingly. Make sure that your customers have enough napkins, utensils, a beverage, and everything that they ordered before they request those items.

Bringing requested items in a timely manner: When a diner asks for extra napkins, bring them quickly. Remember, if they ask for something that is not on their table, you've already failed. Your diners shouldn't need to ask for a utensil, napkin, or a refill. However, when they ask, bring the items quickly to recover from your customer service snafu.

Upselling with a smile: Part of this tactic is knowing the menu well. What pairs well with each menu item? Does the local Riesling pair well with the Chicken special? Would you suggest a certain dessert with their port wine? If you love the homemade hash browns, suggest it with a smile. There is a two-fold goal in upselling with a smile. First, suggesting and upselling a great dish will enrich your customers' lives. Second, the added revenue and great suggestion will increase your gratuities. However, please don't upsell any item unless you are passionate about it.

Serving customers correctly or not "selling:" "Selling" is asking customers what they ordered when you bring their food. It reminds me of an auctioneer at an auction house, "Who has the fish? Who has the fish? Asking once, twice, sold to the lady in the red dress? Now who has the steak au poivre?" "Selling" is unprofessional and interrupts the natural flow of the dining experience.

Do you have a great memory for lists? If you do, memorize your customers' orders. If not, write it down. Either way, you must record or memorize what each of your diners have ordered. When you place the correct dish in front of your customer without interrupting their revelry or serious conversation, they will reward you with greater wealth. When you interrupt a customer or an entire table with questions about who ordered the diet soda, we know that you are not serious about your job and you care little for our dining enjoyment. Increase your tips by gently recalling the specific order while you place the item in front of them. "Here is the eggplant parmigiano for you, and here is my personal favorite, Penne Arrabbiata. The broccoli di rapa will be ready in a few minutes. Enjoy your meal."

If there is a chance that another server, runner, manager, or busboy will be bringing food or beverages to your table, write an easy description of the person receiving the dish, respectfully, next to their meal. For example, the following descriptions, "woman in red dress (Talapia), man in green shorts (Rigatoni), little girl with ponytail (mac & cheese)," will help the server remember which dish each customer ordered without "selling" them. Be careful to keep the descriptions respectful of your customers. There is a great danger that the diner may see the ticket.

Refilling beverages without customer requesting: Kill your customer with kindness. That first time that you continue to refill their water or soda glass and the customer exclaims with gratitude and fear, "No thank you. I'm all set," you've created a grateful customer for life.

Removing empty plates and glasses at the appropriate time: There is great controversy about this practice. There are many schools of thought concerning the proper time to remove empty plates from the table. The traditional and preferred way is to remove excess items from the table when everyone at the table has finished their meal. If you start removing plates from the table and the other diners are not finished, you have created a pocket of discomfort. The unfinished diners may feel rushed and embarrassed by this. They don't want to inconvenience their fellow diners, so they may ask for you to remove their plates even if they haven't finished.

Another option is to be cognizant of the comfort level of the individual diners of each table. If a customer is pushing their plates far away, placing their utensils in the four o'clock position, and have placed their dirty napkin onto the plate, they're absolutely finished. You are ruining their dining experience if you don't remove their plates.

As you slowly add each of the above techniques of growing your gratuities, remember that it's possible to earn an entire shift's possible tips from one table. I have often earned tips as high as 50-100% of the total bill. I've been tipped $50 just for bringing a couple to their table. On a $200 restaurant bill, they were grateful for my customer service and left $100 for me, and $100 for the bartender. Even during a slow shift with few customers, you can earn as much as other busier shifts.

3

Missed Opportunities

Our family is indecisive in choosing a restaurant. Lisa and I have spent over 25 years, sometimes literally, standing on a street corner asking ourselves, "where do you want to eat?" When we lived in New York, we'd ask, "Do you want Chinese, Mexican, Italian, Thai, pizza, dairy, meat?" Then we would say aloud the various choices for each category. Fast forward to the present and we have instilled in our children the same level of indecisiveness. One Sunday night, almost all of us wanted Italian food. In Michigan, most restaurants close early on Sunday evening and so we were left with few choices. The restaurant's website and social media sites all pointed to a 9 p.m. closing time. We walked in at 8pm, the restaurant was virtually empty except for 2 couples on separate tables. One of the co-owners walked towards us without a smile, somberly shaking his head. I thought that maybe something terrible happened in the kitchen. No, the co-owner tells us that they are closed because they don't have many customers tonight. I wasn't shocked because although the food is wonderful there, the service is always terrible. During a previous visit, we had a similar situation at this restaurant when we were greeted by the somber owner five minutes after we entered. The chef was embarrassed that we waited so long, and that's why he notified the owner that we were at the door.

If you ask yourself why a certain restaurant is never crowded, the answer is that they have a serious customer service disease.

Another great sin of retail is closing before the advertised closing time. You have no idea how much money you lose when you close early or rush customers out of your shop. For the neighborhood bake shop that bakes everything fresh daily and closes traditionally when they have nothing else to sell, this of course, doesn't apply. When you close early because of lack of fresh baked product to sell, we'll value your product highly and blame ourselves if we forget to come earlier!

Closing early will cause your business to fail. When you fail your customers, they will rush into the arms of another similar business. In this case, we dined next door. We spent $150 in food and beverages and tipped the server $30 because the service was excellent. If the first restaurant seated us with a smile, they would have been at least $200 richer and perhaps, if they seated our lovely young family of five by the window, other customers would have dined there. They had the potential of making enough money to cover the earlier slow hours. They will never know and as they alienate enough customers, they will eventually close.

There is too much competition in the restaurant industry. Your food can be mediocre, but if you have extraordinary customer service, customers will return and tell their friends. Great food with terrible customer service will kill your business. With great food and great customer service, you will never fail. This Italian restaurant lost on my recommendations and referrals. Chazzano Coffee customers ask me frequently, "where should I have lunch?" I will never recommend this Italian restaurant because I fear that my customers will be mistreated. Therefore, the restaurant is losing thousands of dollars just from me.

On a positive note, customers call Chazzano Coffee Roasters often a few minutes before our advertised and well-known closing time. "Could you stay open just until 6:10 p.m.? We're a few minutes away." Do you know why we almost always say "yes?" There are many reasons to stay open later. The fact that a customer is rushing to buy from us is incredibly humbling. They love our product so much that they must acquire it before tomorrow. When we stay open for customers later than advertised, they will always tell their friends about the great customer service at Chazzano Coffee Roasters. They will personally bring their friends to the shop, tell their co-workers, and will share their love of Chazzano with every coffee lover they meet.

The fundamental axiom of customer service is: make it easy for customers to buy from you.

Another customer service sin committed by this restaurant owner is "lack of hunger for new customers." Who cares if you want to go home early? Aren't you hungry for new customers? If you own a café and a few customers walk in a few minutes before closing, find a way to make a sale. Let them know that you close in a few minutes, tell them when you reopen tomorrow, and give them a free beverage to go.

Think of customer experience as speed dating: make a great first impression and try to convince them that you're worthy of a second date.

4

Using entertainment in your restaurant or café

One of our favorite restaurants has great food, but the food is "expertly crafted." That is another way of saying that the food is placed in front of us about 25-45 minutes after we order. During this eternal wait for our food, I wonder if I'll ever get served. There aren't enough appetizers to keep me from starving. I drink about 20 glasses of soda before the food arrives. There are various television screens, but there's nothing to do. When I dine with friends or family, I feel really strange that I brought them to a restaurant with this incredibly long wait. At the neighborhood pizzeria, you can watch the pizza makers prepare the pizza, open and close the ovens, or spin the pizza over their heads. They are often very friendly with their customers and you may be entertained by that conversation. In other restaurants, there are board games, or at least a bread basket with three different kinds of olive oil.

Entertaining your customers while they wait is an art form and as such needs to be part of your customer service- you need to plan out your improvisation. At a local Greek restaurant, you'll hear "Opa" shouted loudly at least every five minutes. The server sets a dish aflame and there's a large flame that shoots up to the ceiling. You believe every time that the ceiling will catch on fire. If you're close by to the flame, you feel your face burning for a fleeting moment. Even if the service is terrible and the kitchen's slow, your hunger will subside every time that you hear "Opa."

There's a brilliant reason for the cheap coloring sets found in chain restaurants. They want to entertain your children while you wait for your food. Once the restaurant fills up, your dining experience will slow down and your children's patience will dissolve.

What do you do to entertain your customers while they wait? Do you know that the simple act of refilling your customers' beverage without conversation is entertaining? I love when a server refills my water without asking. I feel like royalty. I often feel like I'm going to explode with all of that liquid, but a waiter that is attentive creates a reassuring experience.

At Chazzano Coffee Roasters, we have many methods of

entertaining customers. Our brewing styles are similar to science experiments. The Vacuum Syphon Brewer with its butane burner, and the iced pourover, can entertain without words. However, we'll still explain everything that we're doing to all present in the café. While we're brewing Turkish coffee, we'll explain: Did you know how many ethnic groups brew coffee the Turkish method? Iranians, Yemenites, Israelis, Turks, Greeks, Chaldeans. Some boil their coffee three times, and some 4; some stir their coffee, some don't; furthermore, some add sugar, rosewater or cardamom and others drink it black. You waited 5-7 minutes for a small cup of Turkish coffee but you weren't bored. Sometimes you are able to entertain with education. Even the French Press is simple, but fancy and entertaining. There's nothing entertaining about pouring coffee from a spigot or from a glass coffee carafe.

At the Rustic Inn, I would entertain my customers by singing while I set the Baked Alaska aflame. I explained how the dessert was made and created a bit of theater or in this case, musical theater with my singing. In addition, we were taught to pour coffee for our customers using a long necked coffee pot and a white ceramic cup. We would begin pouring the cup of coffee slowly. As the coffee was poured into the cup, we moved the cup and coffee pot about 3 feet away from each other while continuing the stream of coffee. The customers surely felt a bit of fear and trepidation, but they were entertained by the drama of a simple cup of coffee. I was also taught how to carry plates on my arm. At one point, I was able to carry 4-5 plates on my arm and 2 on the other hand. When I passed you with 4-7 plates on my arms, I entertained you and enriched your experience. On the other hand, if you carry a tray of plates to my table, I'm not entertained. It just seems lazy.

There's a Mexican restaurant that is not traditional and doesn't serve the best food. However, when you order the guacamole, the server brings out all of the ingredients and mixes them in front of you. Guacamole is basically mashed avocado with tomato and cilantro. Yet, we appreciate the gesture of the mortar and pestle brought to our table for our entertainment.

Many years ago, before kids, my brother-in-law and sister-in-law brought us to an Indian restaurant. For three hours, (I'm not lying), we sat on cushions on the floor, and were served a small dish every 15 minutes. We were mesmerized by the music, the various ways that the food was plated, and the different experience of sitting on the floor and eating with our hands. Now that we have kids, I would only go to this Indian restaurant if I hated myself, but it was one of the most memorable dining experiences.

Do you hear that? Neither do I. That's the sound of silence. It's more painful than bad music or loud music. If you own any business, except for a funeral home, please have some sounds emanating from the speakers. If there's a hell, and not Hell, Michigan, it's when the master of the gates of hell makes you wait for eternity in complete silence.

5

The diner's bill of expectations

There should be a Bill of Expectations for diners. What should diners expect from their restaurant experience? Are there some inalienable rights that should kick in once one walks into a café or restaurant? Yes, and here they are:

1. I expect to be greeted with a smile immediately upon entering the restaurant. If there are other customers around, I expect you to turn your head slightly, and say hello and tell me that you'll soon help me.

2. I expect that if you're not able to help me immediately, that you communicate the timetable for your responsiveness.

3. I expect that you speak honestly with me from the time that you first see me until the time that I leave your shop.

4. I expect to be seated at a clean table.

5. I expect that you will quickly speak with me when I'm seated.

6. I expect that you will know the menu well and have your personal recommendations available.

7. I expect that my food or beverages will arrive in a reasonable amount of time.

8. I expect that when my food arrives, that you will not ask who will receive each particular item. You will place the item in front of the correct customer without inconveniencing them and ask, "Is there anything else I can bring?"

9. I expect that you will monitor our table and decide on whether we are finished with a plate by the placement of our fork and knife. I expect that you will remove the plates, if possible, from the right hand side, and place new plates from the left hand side.

10. I expect that you will not ask us any questions while we are in a conversation or chewing.

11. I expect that you will frequently look at us to ascertain whether we need anything without interrupting our conversation or our enjoyment of the dining experience.

12. I expect that you will refill our water glass without asking, and ask if we would like another beverage.

13. I expect that our bill will be available soon after requesting it and our payment will be processed soon afterward.

14. I expect that you will again smile as we leave your establishment and say either "Have a great day" or "Thank you for coming in."

6

Who is your GFI officer?

There would be peace in the world if first impressions were all perfect. How many times have you walked into a retail shop and were ignored for several minutes? I walked into a nearly empty café that serves Chazzano Coffee with my three children and was ignored for five minutes. How many times have you waited on the phone until the next customer service representative was available? Bad first impressions will ruin your business or your livelihood as a server. Every store needs a GFI officer, or a Great First Impressions officer. Is your receptionist smiling at your customers and making them feel welcome? Is the hostess saying hello to your customers immediately and with a smile? When your restaurant is busy, who is greeting the onslaught of customers? I suggest that you have one person who is the chief Great First Impressions officer to make sure that everyone in your employ knows how to greet customers. However, every one of your employees needs to understand how to greet customers with alacrity.

In healthy and organized restaurants, there's a chain of command. The host greets the customers, asks how many are in the group, and then seats them at a table. They will then tell you that the server will be with you shortly. The host may even make you feel welcome by bringing over a beverage of your choice from the bar. The server should arrive quickly to take your beverage order or will at least share that she will return shortly to take your order. However, all of the other employees in the restaurant should be killing you with kindness by saying hello.

As a server or host, when you notice that the server is late coming to their new table, walk over to the table and say with a smile, "your server will be right with you." You might even, with the manager's permission, take their beverage order or just bring water to their table. If the restaurant fosters a healthy and friendly atmosphere amongst the servers, you should whet their appetite by sharing with them the specials of the day.

The most important aspect of enthusiastic first impressions is that the customer should feel like the mere act of walking into your shop can cure cancer or bring peace to the world. Your customers should say after that first impression, "Thank you for making me feel welcome." All of your staff should turn towards a new customer and say, "hello we'll be right with you."

In every Italian restaurant, Lisa and I find the table farthest from the front door. Why? We learned from mafia movies, when a hit man comes in firing a machine gun to "wipe you out," you need to see them coming and duck underneath the table. (What that will accomplish, I have no idea, but it seems to work in the movies.) This is our private joke. Even the kids don't know what we're doing. Whomever is forced to sit with their back to the front door will receive a knowing smirk that says, "You're in trouble." Why am I telling this somewhat humorous story? I hope that you know the answer.

Guard the door with your life or as if the life of your business depends upon it. Your employees, whether baristas, hosts, servers or receptionists, should be vigilantly guarding and watching the door. Guarding against what, you ask? Guarding against the possibility that a client or customer will enter your establishment and not feel welcomed during the first few seconds. After a few seconds, you've failed. Truly. When I walk into a business searching desperately for a happy, smiling, and welcoming face, you've lost me. I'll probably buy from you now because I'm here, but I won't return.

The one guarding the door must have a happy soul or be a great actor. Teach your employees to acquire that happy soul. Teach them to be genuine in their enthusiasm about the business. Even funeral homes are welcoming.

Guarding the door involves specific responsibilities:

1. Making sure the customer will be served soon.

2. Making sure the customer is thanked profusely before they leave your establishment.

Remember that the first person who welcomes a new customer is the one who will be remembered for their kindness. You helped that person feel like a part of the community. They will be forever grateful.

Create a SOP (standard operating procedure) for greeting customers.

1. The approved way of answering the phone that corresponds to your type of business.

2. How do you address customers when they walk into your store?

3. How soon after the door opens do you say hello?

4. Who is responsible for welcoming and greeting customers or clients? (everyone)

5. What is the chain of command? Who should take care of this customer?

7

Keeping it real

During all of the episodes of "Jersey Shore," the residents of the insane asylum would use every curse word imaginable. This was true also in my Italian family. Every family conversation whether in anger or joy was laced with expletives. Saying some special words that rhymed with "truck" and "fit" weren't necessarily bad words in my family. On "Jersey Shore," these words weren't terrible either, they were part of normal speech. However, the worst words that you could say to someone on "Jersey Shore," were "You're fake!" This was powerful because some of the guys and gals on the show were "fake" in appearance with excessive make-up, body enhancements, and their favorite daily past-time was GTL (Gym, Tanning, Laundry). Calling someone "fake" meant that they weren't being real. They were lying, they weren't being true to themselves and they were losing who they were as a person.

It's necessary to keep it real in your life. Are you willing to be the "real" you? Are your present circumstances shaping you in a way that "you're fake?" If you're selling something that you do not feel passionately about or you don't believe in, you are a fake. I love going to small family owned restaurants to dine because they are real. They're selling their family owned products about which they are passionate. They won't sell something to you they are trying to get rid of. Instead, they'll sell something they personally love to eat.

As a server in a restaurant, keep it real. Sell the food that you personally love. As a barista in a café, sell the café related products that you love. If you don't love matcha lattes, don't recommend them. We will know that you're being fake. At Chazzano Café, the matcha lattes are very popular, but I wouldn't recommend them because I love our Matcha, but not with milk. Don't accept a job when you don't believe in the product or service that you're selling. If you're selling mortgages, and you hate the job, and you hate the company, you're not going to sell well. In addition, your health and happiness will also suffer. Find a way to keep it real. Be yourself.

Do you know how thrilled I am when a server tells me to choose one product over another? When we dine at a restaurant with a great wine selection, I'll ask the server: "Which wine is your favorite?" I truly love when the server says, "Yes, we sell a lot of this wine, but it's not my favorite."

I want the server to help enrich my life by sharing what she loves most. If the server likes a particular entree, I'm sure that the chef cooks it with love. Customers buy more from honest people who care about them. If you love only one thing on the menu, share that information with me.

8

The power of suggestion

I walked all the way into a shop that serves Chazzano Coffee for the first time. I walked all the way into the shop, into the bathroom, without anyone acknowledging my existence. Lest you believe that I'm interested in speaking about great first impressions, that is for another chapter. In this chapter, I will discuss lost opportunities or on a positive note, how powerful suggestions with a smile will grow your business or create greater wealth for servers. Yes, the hostess committed the grave sin of bad first impressions, but the greatest sin here was a lack of education. When I paid for my food, she was brewing her first pot of Chazzano Coffee for the store. I was waiting for her to share what she was doing. If she shared with me (shop owner disguised as Joe customer) that this coffee was roasted by a local roaster, and that she was brewing a fresh pot of coffee now, I would have purchased a cup. If she brought the bag over to me and invited me to smell the delicious aromatics of this fresh roasted coffee, It would have brought a smile to my face. When a business makes me smile or improves my life, I will force myself to return even if it is inconveniently located. If other customers were around in the shop (alas, it was empty), they would have sold out of the first pot of coffee. In addition, those customers would have asked about this Chazzano Coffee Roasters shop. The customers would be thrilled that you introduced them to a great cup of coffee, but also introduced them to a new, cool business.

When I recommend a certain coffee to one customer in my café, I speak clearly so that other customers can hear my recommendation and I will look around and find out who else is listening to this conversation. With my eyes, I will scan the café and look at other customers who are listening in. When I speak about a certain coffee that tastes like praline, marzipan, and is nutty and buttery, the other customers will ask me about that coffee. After the initial sale to the original customer, the other customers will ask for a pound of that coffee on their way out. With one conversation meant for one customer, I was able to create four other customers. The original sale was around $20. Now, I've quadrupled that sale with the power of suggestion. To be absolutely clear, what creates this exponential sale is my honesty and passion for my coffee and my sincere desire to enrich my customers' lives.

The power of suggestion is one ingredient of excellent customer service and for increasing your gratuities. When you approach one of your tables and explain the specials of the day, speak just a bit louder than usual so that your other tables may hear the specials. Have those specials memorized and make sure that you have a favorite. Your favorite special will sell more than the other choices. Why do you love that special item? Does the watermelon appetizer sprinkled with balsamic vinegar remind you of your summer vacations? Humanize and create honest, real stories about the products on the menu. If there is a smile on your face, a smile in your eyes, and you speak well and with passion, your original customers will buy from you and the customers overhearing your conversation will be intrigued. I have spoken elsewhere and frequently about the importance of educating your customers, but this power of suggestion is a different level. If you suggest a certain wine that you believe pairs well with their chosen entree, your customer will accept your suggestion and tip you well.

We love drinking new previously unknown wines. I will often ask for a wine recommendation from the server. She'll ask, "Do you want a red or white? Bold or light?" Sometimes they'll realize that I know a little bit more and ask, "Do you want something fruit forward or high tannins?" The most successful servers have a few favorites that they share with me. Some will even recommend that I don't choose a certain wine because the flavor profile is uninteresting. If you help me find an available wine that will pair well with my meal, you have my eternal gratitude. You've enriched my life, educated me, and provided some entertainment. During this conversation if you spoke a bit louder, other customers may order this wine that you recommended.

You're sitting at the café enjoying your first cup of Chazzano Coffee. "How's the coffee?" we ask. You reply, "It's great. Thank you!" We suggest, "If you have a lazy hour and a half someday, you might want to try 'Drinking for the Cycle.' That's when you try the same single origin coffee in 6 different ways: French Press, Iced, Vacuum Syphon, Espresso, Pourover, and Turkish. Bring a friend." When a new couple comes to the café, we'll suggest a "coffee flight" of 4 different coffees. Again, this added information is not only for the original customer. We're planting seeds for future visits from all of the customers present.

Here's a suggestion for most fast food operations: make a suggestion. How many times have you stood in front of a fast food menu with the huge amount of selections paralyzed with indecision? There are several fast food chains that we've visited at least twenty times and where we still take forever to decide. Which vegetarian soup should we have? Should I get the soup and sandwich or just the sandwich? The tomato and mozzarella panini or the tuna sub? I would probably die of shock if the cashier of the fast food store shared a suggestion. How wonderful if the lovely woman at the counter said, "Do you know what's my favorite? The tuna sandwich with honey mustard on a baguette. That's my favorite lunch sandwich." How many people waiting in line would order that sandwich? Most of them would, but even if they didn't, the lovely woman at the counter, you, made the line move quicker.

Have you noticed the various associates at your favorite local specialty market in each of the aisles? They are waiting to provide you with a suggestion about their favorite local roaster, favorite wine or cheeses, or favorite deli item. There are too many choices of each item in the supermarket. It's impossible for us to adequately research all of our choices. We need the cashier, counter person, server, or customer service representative to make suggestions.

Your favorite local wine shop also uses the power of suggestion. Sure, they'll ask you many questions about what kind of wine you usually enjoy, but you will probably choose the wine they suggest most emphatically. "Those are all great wines, but this is my favorite." I almost guarantee that you'll choose that wine.

Use the power of suggestion physically by bringing the dessert plates to your customers slowly so that other customers will interrupt their concentration and look at the beautifully plated desserts. A customer who is completely full with no impetus to order dessert will often ask his fellow diners, "Would you like to share a dessert?" If you have a special way of serving your food or what I call food entertainment, use the power of suggestion to replicate sales of that item. At the café, when we brew coffee in the lab experiment like Vacuum Syphon, we'll elevate it or even serve it at the table so that more customers are able to watch. Of course, many of the other customers will ask, "What is that? How is coffee brewed in that thing different from a French Press?" So, we've educated our customers, entertained them, and used the power of suggestion to create repeat sales of this product or service.

The power of suggestion will grow your revenue, educate your customers, and build an army of repeat customers.

9

Thou shalt not hand a plate to a customer

The greatest sin of mankind is not hatred, prejudice, or violence, it is the act of handing a plate to a customer. I can hear the angels screaming, "No, don't do that! That family came to the restaurant to be served their food. They don't want to bus their own table and hold a plate of hot food. You're ruining the fabric of etiquette!"

Many restaurants have filled their space with more tables than is possible to properly serve their customers. Unless it's impossible to serve correctly, don't hand plates to the customer. Walk around them with a smile and gently place the plates in front of them without displacing them or without interrupting their conversation. When we dine out, we expect that the server will hand us a plate of food or at least attempt it. This practice is lazy and will hurt your customers' experience. When customers dine out, they want to be served and they want to be treated like kings.

Keep the customer out of the service industry. I am an obnoxious diner. If and when a server hands me the plate, I will ignore them and wait until they get the message that they need to place the plate in front of me. I have no desire to touch the plate and do the server's work. However, if a restaurant is crowded and it's impossible for the server to reach around me, I expect you to say, "I apologize for handing you the plate, could you please pass this down?"

10

Thou Shalt Not Put Your Fingers on My Plate

Thou shalt not touch your hair or face or scratch any part of your body

Please don't place your fingers or finger nails on my plate anywhere next to my food. Serve me a cup or glass either by touching the saucer or bottom of the glass. Do not put your fingers or hands near the place that my mouth touches. If you break these rules, my brain then imagines and questions whether you wash your hands after using the bathroom. Are you touching your hair when you go back to the kitchen?

After you bussed the sick lady's plate at the next table, did you wash your hands? In fact, I'm running through all of the worst scenarios that could have occurred. Really, I'm imagining where your fingers have been during your entire lifetime. Therefore, you have ruined my meal because I have stopped enjoying the meal with my family and I've begun to dream about your improper hygienic habits. Even as I write this, I am not enjoying my cup of coffee because even though you are the proverbial bad server, I can imagine all of the worst scenarios. Don't touch my food. Please.

Yes, this is a long negative commandment, but I just want to emphasize the pain that I experience when you describe the appetizer while touching your nose. Or when you bring my glass of wine and then put your fingers through your hair. Or when you scratch your abdomen when you tell me about the specials. If you were my employee, I'd send a message to you to wash your hands immediately. The issue is that I don't know whether you are going to wash your hands, ever. I don't know how high is your understanding of personal hygiene. Instead, I expect you to get more involved with your nose after you go to the kitchen. I expect you to fix your hair while you're in the kitchen, waiting for my food. My imagination will go wild and then you'll ruin my entire meal when you place your fingers too close to the tip of my wine glass, or when your finger accidentally touches my side dish of broccoli. Again, this is about entertainment. Anyone who has ever worked in a restaurant knows that there are so many unsavory activities that would ruin the possibility that you dine out ever again. However, I want secrecy and illusion. I don't want to know that the sous chef just sneezed into the large bowl of the special soup of the day and didn't tell anyone. I can't control what I can't see. However, help me with the illusion that I'm being treated like royalty at your establishment.

Make a pact with yourself. Every time you touch your hair, face, or any other body part I haven't discussed, wash your hands. If you must wash your hands with ridiculous repetition, you will stop with this unhygienic behavior. If you must know, your gratuity depends upon your hygiene.

11

Thou shalt not stack plates

Why does stacking plates disturb me so? It's lacking creativity and there's no sense of entertainment. If the server placed five plates along the entire length of his arm and walked successfully to the kitchen, that would be ideal. Unfortunately, no one is comfortable doing that entertainment because they're not trained. Instead, stack one plate at a time along your arm. Don't remove every plate at the same time. Return to the table a few times to remove a few more plates and glasses.

There is also the negative visual aspect of stacking plates at the table. The unpleasant noise of hearing plates hitting plates muffled by the mashing of all of our meals will ruin the meal, creating the impossibility of ordering dessert, and will hurt your gratuities. As I am able to picture this grotesque scene, I see, with abject horror, as the mashing of our entrees spill over the plates. The diners just enjoyed a great meal, with attentive service by you, and then they are punished by watching you create all of their left overs into a "mashed" creation. Stacking plates at the table is unappetizing for the diner. In addition, as a server, manager, or owner, create experiences that are rare and special that will leave long lasting memories.

12

Thou shalt not argue with customers

This is a true story. We bought an online coupon for this Italian restaurant that we were dying to visit. When we arrived, it took forever for us to be seated, to be greeted, or to be served. But the fact that we were ignored wasn't the worst sin that occurred. Nor was the incredible fact that the Italian restaurant ran out of pizza and Italian bread. What was most remarkable is that the server was engaging in an angry argument with a four top next to us. The diners were clearly angry. I don't remember the details about their anger, but I remember how rudely the server was speaking to them. He was arguing with an already angry customer. There is no reason to argue with customers. It will ruin your business, cause you to lose your job, and create an eternal well of bad will towards the business. The customers around you will expect you to speak disrespectfully to them. All of the customers will provide poor reviews for your establishment. There are no possible scenarios that could ever warrant arguing with a customer. If they say that they ordered an item, and you disagree (privately), just say, "I apologize. I will bring that item out immediately." If they say that they ordered the item cooked in a certain way, and you disagree with them (privately), just say, "I apologize. I will bring out the item cooked as you ordered."

13

Thou shalt not interrupt

I decided to drive to your café, spend more money than I should, so that I may have a conversation with a business friend, my wife, or I just want to complete some work on the book that I'm writing. You, the server, are very friendly. Perhaps you're too friendly. That's great. I appreciate the warm smile that you presented me when I entered the café. I love how quickly we were served and well...you're doing everything correctly, but you keep interrupting my conversation or my feeble thoughts. Every time that you pass by, you'll engage in small talk: How's the food? How is the cappuccino? May I bring another soda? May I take that plate away?

All of those questions are perfect, but they need to be timed well or your constant interruptions will cause me to lose a sale, forget my train of thought for my writing, or damage my one chance in a long time to have a romantic date with my wife. Please don't interrupt. As you pass by with your winning smile, look to see if we need anything at my table. Judge whether we are in the middle of a conversation or we were looking for you. If we lock eyes as you pass my table and I need anything, I will surely make my request.

I understand that there are times that you must interrupt. Small, quick statements that may interrupt my conversation but behooves me to listen include either "Your food will be right out," or "I apologize, the chef just notified me that we no longer have the Peking Duck tonight, may I suggest another dish?" The first statement doesn't take me away from my conversation. I will be grateful and return to my conversation. The second statement about a change in the menu is important enough to pause.

It should be possible for you to take our complete order except for dessert and coffee at the beginning, serve us our meal and beverages, and then leave us to enjoy ourselves until the end of the meal. After the initial conversation with you, I should be able to carry on my conversation while you place the correct dish in front of the correct diner. We'll all pause and say, "Thank you," but we'll continue with our laughing, our sales call, or our writing.

Just, please don't ask any questions when my mouth is full. If you do, then I will rush to complete my mastication in a pantomime way, wipe my mouth, and then keep you waiting for awhile. I don't want to keep you waiting and if I needed something I would've stopped eating when I first saw you.

Use common sense when serving customers. There are certain times that we're glad that you interrupted us. We're on a bad date, the person we're meeting with is slightly insane, or our conversation will still survive if you interrupt us. When the owner or manager comes over to us to ask, "How is everything?," that's okay. We love when the owner says hello to us. They're busy, but they're taking the time to visit with us. Some managers will just quickly pass by and say, "Thank you for coming in." That doesn't need any acknowledgment except for a "thank you" or "my pleasure."

14

Small Talk

As a supreme master of small talk, it behooves me to share my secrets and why small talk is central to the health of your café or restaurant. Small talk makes your customers feel comfortable and gives them ownership and makes them feel as if they are part of the family. Here are the many phrases that you'll hear me say in almost every social situation.

"Hello, nice to see you!"

Why? Because it is great to see you. You're a customer, perhaps a regular customer, and I want to see you often. It's great for business and it's great for you. I really do mean it when I say that it's nice to see you. In addition, seeing you often at the café means that we're doing something well. We are enriching your life and you see a benefit in being our customer.

"Hello, how are you?"

Again, I really want to know. Why? I may understand why you look depressed or like you're the happiest person alive. I will be able to serve you better. If you're depressed, I might suggest comfort food or something that will make you smile. I hope. If you're happy, you'll probably splurge on dessert or a nice glass of wine. I'm guessing about those choices, but I'll serve you better and provide the respite that you need.

"What's new?"

This is one of my favorite questions because it is completely open ended. By answering this question, you will also answer the "How are you?" question. With this question, I may learn about your passions, hobbies, your business, and in short, what makes you special. Remember, that this question is for regular customers, only.

"What are you doing this weekend? Anything exciting?"

You may not feel comfortable with this question. In addition, the answer may be too long. Whenever you ask a question, make sure that you have the time for the answer. If you're a barista and there are only a few customers at the bar, then ask this question with impunity. However, if you know that the customer is not capable of ceasing the conversation when a new customer comes in, then don't ask the question!

"It looks like a beautiful day!" or "What a beautiful day!"

This is one of the most innocuous statements or questions possible. If the weather is absolutely horrendous, I might say "What beautiful weather we have today" to bring a smile to my customer's face. It's especially funny in a place like Michigan where the weather changes every few minutes. All of the small talk is designed to create a cozy atmosphere for the customer. You're creating the illusion of camaraderie, finding common ground to relax them, and make them feel at home in your place of work.

Cheat Sheet of introductory Small Talk phrases:

1. Hello, nice to see you.

2. Hello, how are you?

3. What's new?

4. What are you doing this weekend? Anything exciting?

5. Great weather we're having today!

Cheat Sheet of Closing Small Talk phrases:

1. Great to see you.

2. Thanks for coming in.

3. Have a great day.

If you insert the person's name, (if you know their name), you have just gained a lifelong customer.

There are negative consequences corresponding to every positive action. For example, small talk is dangerous if you talk too much about yourself. Keep your answers short and sweet. The customer often doesn't really want to know what you are doing this weekend. They are asking you because they are polite. If you begin telling them about your yogi and how you want to move to India to learn proper yoga techniques, you've just lost a customer. They will do everything in their power to never be served by you again. They will look through the window to see if you're working today. Truthfully, you are their server, not their friend. They want to be served with class and they are willing to pay well for competency, flair, and respect.

15

In the Weeds

Have you every been "in the weeds?" When you're in the weeds, it's as if you are in a large field and the weeds are way above your head and you can't see where you're going. You don't know which direction to go and what is the most important thing to do immediately. In the customer service world it's when you have a seemingly insurmountable amount of customers at the same time and you have no idea how to serve them all and provide excellent customer service. You've seen servers in restaurants who are in the weeds. They're perspiring profusely, they look nervous. They're speaking with you, but you can almost hear their private thoughts: "Did they just put another couple in my station?" They feel like quitting because they don't see any way out of the weeds. They're crying inside, "Please, God, please make this stop!"

Besides the perspiration on their scalp, another sign of a server who is *in the weeds* is when they are constantly looking down. In their panic, they are praying, "Maybe some of the customers will go away if I don't acknowledge them." They're making one beverage at a time. Every time they lift their head, more customers come through the door. They have not been trained on how to handle a rush of customers. If the server asked several groups of customers at a time what they wanted, they may be able to fill orders quickly. If four different customers want a large coffee to go, wouldn't it make sense to brew them all together, gather the four cups at the same time and maybe cash them out together? It sure would.

You'll never know that if you keep your head down and process orders one at a time. If you knew that there were six different orders for lattes, small and large, wouldn't it save time to brew all of the espresso shots at the same time, steam the milk at the same time, and process their orders at the same time? Suddenly, you're no longer "in the weeds" because everyone has at least part of their order in front of them. The customers know that you're busy, but now they're impressed with you. You smiled throughout that secretly painful ordeal, processed orders quickly, and made everyone happy. You've created happy soon-to-return customers, created wealth for the company and for you (in tips), and you've gained a life-long skill of learning to turn *in the weeds* into a *controlled slam*.

When I was a server in various restaurants, but especially at the Rustic Inn in Annapolis, Maryland, and Lucky's Grill in NYC, I learned techniques to turn a potential *in the weeds* situation to a *controlled slam*. For example, when you have 10 tables, treat them as one table- treat them as if it's a family dinner. If everyone realizes that you know that they exist, they will understand if it takes a longer time. Never pass a table without looking at your customers in the eyes. Say hello, ask if everything is okay, but look at them and smile. They may need a fork because their fork fell on the floor. As you pass every table, force yourself to spy on all of your occupied tables. Make sure that everyone has a beverage. Do triage and make the situation manageable.

My café is frequently busy and when we are slammed, and not "in the weeds," we treat the 30 customers that come in as one table. While we help each customer, one at a time, when another customer comes in we say, "Hello, how are you? We'll be right with you." I'll even introduce them to each other so that they forget that they waited 10 minutes for a cup of coffee. When we take care of one customer, we're constantly looking around with a smile, saying, "we'll be right with you." The smile and constant communication is the key to turning an experience "in the weeds" to just being crazy busy or slammed. "Slammed" is when a plethora of customers enter your establishment at the same time and they all feel that they have been taken care of.

Another technique to change *in the weeds* into a *controlled slam* is through free samples. "I'll be with you in a moment, would you like a sample of our new coffee, Colombia Villa Maria Caldas Supremo? It has notes of peanut butter." Not only will your waiting customers be grateful, but they may even purchase bags of this coffee. In a restaurant, make sure that your many customers all have something to drink. Frequent refills are great, but diners soon catch on that you're doing that to make them forget that their food has not arrived in a timely manner. Their viciously growling hunger pains will remind them of this ruse. Communicate the honest expected arrival of their next course. Explain why the course has not arrived. Is the entree freshly prepared? Does it take the steak longer to cook? Of course, all of that information should be provided when they place their orders.

One solution to getting out of the weeds is to treat "too many customers at one time" as one table or create the illusion that the customers are in your home, just hanging out and waiting for their food. Think about when you go to a friend's house for a dinner party. When you are greeted at the door, they'll help you with your coat, and then they'll ask "what do you want to drink?" If there are other friends present, the host isn't going to make your drink and then ask one other friend what they'd like! The host will ask, what can I get for all of you? Then they'll bring out every drink at the same time. At this point, we forget about how long we're waiting for food because we have a beverage and we're having a conversation with someone at the dinner party.

There lies the next part of getting out of the weeds: creating conversations with customers or introducing customers to one another. "Bob, do you know Greg? Bob owns Acme Corp. and Greg owns a lighting store." Then Bob and Greg say hello to one another, strike up a conversation, and they soon forget about the time. Other customers soon join in and no one is paying attention to the time needed to fill all of the orders. At our café, we'll ask if the customer has a few minutes. If they are ordering very slow coffee like Turkish coffee which takes more than five minutes, we'll explain the expected brewing time.

I remember a morning at Chazzano when we were slammed because we make "fancy" coffee. No one is upset about the time it takes when you are brewing coffee in a fancy brewer like a pour-over, vacuum syphon, iced pourover, or Turkish. The show becomes part of the entertainment. When I worked at the Rustic Inn, and I was neglecting a few tables while setting the Baked Alaska aflame with Grand Marnier, no one was fidgety or angry that they couldn't get their check or dessert. They appreciated the show. The same scenario happens at my café. There are twenty people waiting, but while we're making 2 Turkish coffees, two vacuum syphons and 3 hot chocolates, customers are entertained. So, customer service is not just dependent on the server, but also dependent on the management providing the proper tools to keep customers comfortable, relaxed and entertained.

16

Training your staff is an eternal endeavor

The only thing that I dislike about being an owner is the simple truth: Training never ends. It is eternal. Set up the best customer service, teach your employees how to educate your customer, and hire happy and motivated employees. Still, if you watch these highly trained employees, you'll realize that they will never understand every single aspect of the training. One employee will start stacking plates. Another employee will reach over the customer. Yet another employee will forget to immediately greet customers when they walk into your shop. There are always pieces of the puzzle that are forgotten. It's not intentional or malicious at all.

There are three reasons for the eternal training of your employees:

1. They don't own the restaurant or café. Their entire life savings were not drained to build this business. They receive a pay check regardless of how they do their jobs or how much the business earns.

2. In the service industry, there is often great turnover of employees returning to college or finding employment elsewhere.

3. Your customer service methods and beliefs will change. There are some fundamental truths, but I hope that every few months or at least every year, you will re-evaluate your customer service Standard Operating Procedure (SOP). As your staff changes, so will your SOP.

We dined at one of our favorite restaurants known for its great service. However, to our chagrin, the new server was stacking plates and "selling" the menu. The server asked, "who gets the cheesecake?" The server reached over one of my children to serve my wife even when the server had enough room to go around me and serve her properly. What happened to the great customer service? Perhaps the chef or owner wasn't around. Perhaps, they haven't had enough time to train their employees before every shift. Was the server new? How do you create consistency in your service? Every time that I dine at this restaurant, I expect spectacular service because the food is expensive. Few will complain about the cost if the customer service and food are both spectacular.

At Lucky's Bar and Grill, a mandatory wine tasting was

conducted at every afternoon training. It was imperative that we knew how the wines tasted and the manager knew that knowledgeable servers would sell more bottles of wine. I often led the contest for the most bottles served because I understood that knowledge is power. I appreciated the discussion about the differences between the various vintners and grape varietals because it translated in selling more bottles of wine which increased my gratuities. In addition, we sampled the specials before every shift (before I started keeping Kosher) and were asked to describe what we were eating.

At another local restaurant, I was privy to a chef training her employees before the dinner shift. Her assistant chef brought out several specials, including a chicken dish that had lemon. The chef tasted the lemon chicken and told the assistant chef, with quiet rage, "you cooked the lemon at the wrong time with the chicken, it needs to be cooked towards the end." Every shift, the servers taste the various specials and the chef discusses the various culinary choices. During this shift, the servers were privy to how special the lemon chicken was for the chef. If you told this story to your diners, imagine how many lemon chicken specials you would sell.

17

The customer is always right unless you have integrity

The customer is always right unless your business has integrity. The customer is always right unless they ask for the perfectly rare fresh tuna to be cooked well done. If the chef has integrity and pride in her menu, she will kindly suggest another dish. Over cooking the tuna will hurt her business and will confuse her customers. At our café, the customer is always right unless they request a mocha latte or for us to put sugar in our coffee. A new chef has recently made the following pronouncement: ketchup is not available for anyone above the age of 10. At first, some might say that the chef is being excessively snobby and elitist. Other chefs will probably applaud his audacity and question their own fear of making such a pronouncement.

As a server, it is your job to uphold the integrity of the café or restaurant. Don't bend the rules because you will eventually be caught. Crime doesn't pay or it doesn't pay for long. There is one crime for immediate dismissal at Chazzano Café: mixing cocoa mix with an espresso based beverage to create a mocha latte. That act is completely against our vision statement: fresh roasted coffee doesn't need sugar, cream or added flavorings. As an employee of Chazzano, you are respected and tipped well because you've upheld the basic tenets of the business. Our target market respects our integrity and will reward our servers for their integrity.

"The customer is always right" is a myth and it has been misused and misunderstood. When a customer orders a latte, and when you bring their latte they exclaim, "Oh, no, I ordered a cappuccino," the customer is right because it's not hurting your integrity. You're just helping create a lifelong and happy customer. If my customer asks us to put sugar in the cup of coffee, the private-I-can't-say-this-out-loud answer is, "How dare you put sugar in fresh roasted awesome coffee!" However, we'll explain why they shouldn't, but if they still request the sugar, we point to the unholy place for sugar and joke, "putting sugar in our coffee makes my hands shake."

We may be the rare café that doesn't sell or allow food in our establishment. Part of the reason is that we are kosher certified and it's too complex, expensive, and fraught with danger to have food. Truly, the main reason is that I want people to enjoy the 1500 possible flavor notes that are found in fresh roasted specialty coffee. I don't allow any food, even Kosher food, in the café because I want you to enjoy your coffee or tea without any enhancements.

18

How to recover when you mess up

It's my recurring nightmare. I was carrying a glass of white wine on a serving tray through the restaurant. My mind began to think about something other than balancing that lone glass on top of my tray. I still remember the situation in slow motion as the white wine tipped over, and poured completely onto a gentleman with a pink polo shirt. I apologized profusely and thankfully he was shocked, but not belligerent. The restaurant manager comped them for some part of their meal. I don't remember exactly what happened because I was completely embarrassed and I sheepishly avoided that table.

Chazzano Coffee Roasters ships coffee throughout the world. If a French Press is broken in transit, we'll immediately ship out a new one and add a small amount of our rare microlots to repair the situation.

As a server or manager, understand how much power you have to repair a broken customer service experience. At a local restaurant, the server charged my account for $322 instead of $32. For several days, that $322 was a pending charge. I'm sure that you would apologize as they definitely did. However, what if that was all the money that you had in the bank? Would you just brush it off? What if it stopped you from paying your rent? Thankfully, we were financially sound at the time. Yet, I haven't dined there since the event because they failed me. They should have offered a free meal for us. The amount of money they will lose from us will be many times more than the $322 they accidentally charged to my account.

At a well-known upscale seafood restaurant, I ordered a diet soda (not pop, I will never say pop, no matter how long we live in Michigan, and I will always be a fan of the New York Mets). I took a sip from the cup and wondered about a large piece of ice with a strange shape that filled my glass. Curious, I pulled it out of my glass and realized that it was a 4-inch shard of glass. Some lazy idiot, (and I'm being nice here), probably scooped out ice with a glass and the glass broke, expectantly. He then tried to remove all of the visible pieces. What happens if you break glass in a large restaurant ice machine? You need to empty out the huge amounts of ice, clean and sanitize the unit, and make absolutely certain that the glass is no longer in the ice machine. Probably fearing for their future employment, they didn't tell anyone about their hopefully temporary insanity, and allowed a server to scoop out ice and a large shard of glass for my soda.

If I had swallowed that piece of glass, I would be writing this book from my private island off the coast of South America or my coffee farm in Harrar, Ethiopia. Instead, I graciously pointed out that I had a large piece of glass in my soda. The server seemed embarrassed, but not alarmed. The manager did nothing except offer to comp our desserts. We didn't order dessert because we were disgusted and shocked by the dismal customer service experience. This is an extreme story, but the secret to great customer service is knowing how to repair the situation when you occasionally fail miserably. I would not have told every one of my friends, future friends, and business friends about that restaurant if they would have repaired the situation. With great fear and humility, they should have comped us the entire meal and then as they apologized profusely as we walked out, they should have offered us a free dinner for two. Out of a terrible situation, with a great repair, we would have told our friends about their great customer service.

At a favorite busy breakfast place, my wife ordered a certain egg dish, probably a vegetarian Eggs Benedict, her favorite. Our three children and I were served our food, but Lisa was not. Lisa said, "I ordered the Eggs Benedict." The server said, "No, you did not." I remember that we all laughed because we were in shock. Even if Lisa didn't order that dish, (she did), the server could have feigned apology and then ordered her food correctly. Again, we won't return to that restaurant because we want to spend our money at a place that enriches us and doesn't call us liars.

Teach your employees how to handle a difficult or broken situation and teach them when to kick the responsibilities for repairing the problem to their supervisors.

19

Parting is Sweet Sorrow

Your future is never what you expected. In the past, servers often worked for the same restaurant for decades as their main career. My maternal grandfather, Max Reiner, emigrated to the United States and proceeded to work as a waiter until the day he died. I've been a paperboy, busboy, waiter, host, bartender, clergy, professional singer, and now owner and business consultant. How will your present job influence your future?

Today, servers rarely stay in the same restaurant for more than six months. If you learn these lessons well, restaurants and cafés will love you and reward you for your seemingly "extra" initiative. Your increasing gratuities will represent how much you've positively influenced and enriched your customers' lives. However, you will probably not remain in the food industry forever. Your future dreams will be realized by living a life committed to great customer service.

If you're reading this book as an owner, I hope that I've changed your life and your business. If your customer service remains at a high level, your business has a greater potential for success and perhaps, expansion. Having a ready smile, learning how to repair a customer service mistake, or learning how to educate your customer will assist you in all of your future dreams.

Your present job may not be your dream job, but you must treat this job as if it's your dream job. Do you know that the next person that you greet at the entrance may be the ticket to that perfect job? If they sense happiness, pride in your job, and integrity, many of your dreams may be fulfilled. However, if they sense that you dislike your job, you have sloppy work habits, or are generally unhappy, customers will leave a poor tip and they will not be interested in your future or in the future of the business in which you work.

"Be all that you can be" was the slogan of the United States Army from 2001-2006. The armed forces continue to entice service oriented individuals who understand that military service can be a stepping stone for higher education, learning important skills, and fulfilling your dreams. In every job, however minor or difficult, "be all that you can be."

20

Being a *dugma* (an example) for your employees and becoming a dream facilitator

I have a peculiar problem lately with my employees. I can't seem to keep many employees for more than one year. The nature of the café and service business lends to this phenomenon because a service job is meant to be a stepping stone towards higher employment. Any of my employees that leave us voluntarily quickly apologize and state how much they love their job, but they have decided to do what they originally were trained to do or something that has been their dream for years.

There are many reasons for their decision and I blame myself for many of the reasons. I hire (mostly) people who have a great attitude about life, a sense of humor, and who are passionate about doing what will bring them joy in life. One awesome past employee had the dream of living in Colorado, living off of the land, and having a longer growing season for her vegetable garden. Another awesome past employee had the dream of becoming a professional hairstylist and trainer. Two present employees are on my potential past employee status radar: One is an awesome singer/musician in a great band and another who has a passion for acting. I allow for flexible schedules for my employees to prepare for their ultimate dreams outside of the café. In addition, I teach them by example that life is short and you need to do whatever is going to bring you the greatest joy. I demonstrate that philosophy with the way I speak to customers and vendors, and the almost perpetual smile on my face. The sheer fact that I'm a full-time business owner, part-time clergyperson, and author/ business consultant is a testament to the fact that you can have it all. It takes time, practice, technique and permission to achieve those many dreams, but you need to start somewhere.

If you have the ability to be not only a dream catcher, but a dream facilitator or collaborator for your employees or friends, that's the greatest gift. However, it makes your employees more short term than you'd like. According to the brilliant Rabbi of the middle ages, Rabbi Moses Maimonides, the highest level of charity is to find a job for someone without the recipient knowing who acquired it for them. I believe that a close second is to assist them with their dreams and become a facilitator of those dreams.

ABOUT THE AUTHOR

Frank is the owner of Chazzano Coffee Roasters in Ferndale, Michigan, a professional Cantor, start-up business consultant for God and Coffee Consulting LLC and the author of "God Cries and An Angel Loses its Wings." Frank is working on his third book, "What do you want to be when you grow up?" Frank and his beautiful wife, Lisa, have three beautiful children.